STILL STANDING

I Caught a Flashback

I am standing at the Metro, selling Street Sense,
When a Marine comes up the escalator.
"Good morning sir.
Have a blessed day," I say.
"Would you like to make a donation for a paper?"
"I would," he says, "but I have no money."
Then he asks, "Are you hungry?"
"Not really," I answer.
"But I'll take something for later."
So he goes into his book sack.
And that's when I catch a flashback . . .
When I see that food.
Who woulda thought it be
Beef sauce and spaghetti?
The one they dropped from the helicopter.
Boom! Boom! It hit the floodwater.
We took it to people who couldn't get nothin' to eat.
Cornbread, Ritz crackers, green peas.
I tell him THANKS!
And he say, "Why you say thanks so good like that?"
I say, "I'm a Katrina survivor. I caught a flashback!"

Gerald Anderson

ABOUT GERALD ANDERSON

GERALD ANDERSON DROPPED OUT OF SCHOOL in seventh grade. At age fifteen, he served time in juvenile detention for stealing. Juvie provided his introduction to drugs. While behind bars, he learned to read and write. He was thirty-seven and had been released from prison three weeks before Hurricane Katrina and the subsequent failure of the levees hit New Orleans. After helping rescue victims of the flooding and his evacuation to Washington, D.C., Anderson returned to drugs, burglary, and prison. In 2013, he discovered a new path; he learned he could earn money selling *Street Sense,* a newspaper written and sold by homeless vendors. That's where he began writing his Katrina story with *Street Sense* editor Susan Orlins. Anderson lives with nine other men in a recovery home in Arlington, Virginia.

ABOUT SUSAN ORLINS

SUSAN ORLINS IS AUTHOR OF *CONFESSIONS OF a Worrywart: Husbands, Lovers, Mothers, and Others.* Her essays have appeared in The *New York Times, Newsday,* The *Pennsylvania Gazette,* and The *Washington Post Magazine* among other journals and anthologies. While an editor at *Moment Magazine,* she received a Rockower Award for her profile of sociolinguist Deborah Tannen. Orlins has performed storytelling at The Moth and SpeakeasyDC and performs stand up comedy at clubs in Washington and New York. She facilitates writing and storytelling workshops for homeless writers in Washington, including at *Street Sense,* where she met author Gerald Anderson. Orlins is the mother of three grown daughters and lives with her beagle in Washington, D.C.

STILL STANDING

how an ex-con found salvation
in the floodwaters of katrina

Gerald Anderson
with Susan Orlins

*For my mother, Wilhemena, my brother Emile,
my sister Yolanda, my nephews Terry and Nate,
my aunt Joann, my grandmother Lavinia,
and for Miss Mary, who was like a mother
and a grandmother to me.*

Rest in peace.

Foreword

I ENTERED A ROOM ON THE SECOND FLOOR OF THE Church of the Epiphany, where the writers group was already underway. It was my first day as a volunteer editor at *Street Sense,* Washington, D.C.'s street newspaper, which is written and sold by homeless vendors. A large, dark-skinned man—wearing a black hoodie, baggy jeans and worn-out running shoes—sat in a corner, hunched over a scrap of paper. When I walked over to him, he looked up.

He told me his name was Gerald Anderson and that he was a Katrina survivor. For the upcoming issue of the paper, he was writing words of appreciation to his customers, who had pooled airline miles to send him back to New Orleans for the first time since he had been evacuated eight years earlier.

"What was it like being back in New Orleans?" I asked.

"One of the best parts was meeting new family members," Gerald told me. "My nieces and nephews are grown now and introduced me to they own families. 'This is my daughter.' 'This is my son.'"

Although he had stopped going to school after seventh grade, Gerald knew how to write. But he liked the idea of my taking notes as he spoke. So I tapped on my laptop, while he told me about laughing with old friends, cooking gumbo, and seeing how his hometown had changed.

After finishing his story for the paper, Gerald told me he had rescued a lot of people during the flooding. I knew immediately he had a big story and a gift for telling it.

The following week I said, "Let's write a series for the paper about your Katrina experience."

Others had approached him about writing his story, and he told me he wanted to think about it. Gerald wasn't ready to trust me. I kept asking, and finally he agreed to meet me at Starbucks near the Gallery Place Metro Station, where he sold his papers.

We pulled a couple of stools up to a counter at the window, I bought two egg salad sandwiches, I opened my laptop, and Gerald began telling me what happened.

That was February, 2014 and he has been telling me his story ever since. Each week at Starbucks, he talks, I type. I ask questions, he answers.

First we chat about what's going on in his world; the drama of his present life overlays the drama of how he used skills he learned in prison to rescue others during Katrina.

When Gerald and I met, he was forty-five years old and had been out of prison for almost a year, one of his longest stretches of freedom since he was fifteen. Here's how the cycle went: drugs, burglary, prison, drugs, selling drugs, prison. Now he was homeless, sleeping on assorted people's floors. One man charged him three hundred dollars a month to sleep on his floor, and then within weeks he locked Gerald out and stole his clothes.

Six months after meeting Gerald, I produced a show called "Homeless Lives: Unforgettable Personal Stories" in which professional actors read homeless people's monologues, created in my writing groups. The program included two of Gerald's pieces.

A week before opening night, Gerald appeared with me on TV to promote the monologue show. Dozens of his newspaper customers, whom he refers to as family, watched the TV program in their offices.

Within a day, they began to outfit Gerald for the night of the show. One woman brought a suit that had belonged to her husband. Another customer bought dress shoes for Gerald. The day before the show, he paid a barber ten dollars to cut his short cornrow braids.

On the night of the performance, after hearing his Katrina story read on stage, Gerald walked out of the theater for several minutes. He later told me he had felt emotional, as though he were right back there in New Orleans, reliving the hurricane, battling chin-high flood-waters to rescue a man "who ain't got no legs."

During the time Gerald and I worked on his Katrina memoir, he twice failed to report to his parole officer, which meant he missed two urine tests for drugs. On one of those days I was with him. Snowflakes as big as gum-balls were falling and he said he didn't want to go that far in the snow. It turned out he had reason to avoid the drug test. Soon after, he was ordered to report to court.

When I walked into the courtroom, Gerald was sitting beside his court-appointed lawyer with his head down. His urine had just tested positive for drugs.

He cried that morning; his tears, he said, reflected the shame he felt for having deceived me as well as others who believed in him. In fact, the judge held up twenty-two letters from Gerald's supportive customers, his "family."

That court appearance was the best thing that could have happened, because instead of sending Gerald back to prison, the judge allowed his parole officer to arrange a bed for him at Phoenix House, a residential drug treatment program. For the next ten weeks, instead of meeting downtown at Starbucks, Gerald and I met every Sunday— visiting day—in a courtyard at Phoenix House in Northern Virginia, where he continued telling me his story.

He progressed so well that in less than three months, he moved to a nearby recovery house, where he currently lives with nine other men.

Three weeks before publishing his memoir, Gerald stood waiting for a subway when a man fell on the tracks. Gerald jumped down to rescue the man, whom others helped pull to the platform. It was steeper than Gerald had realized, and the others helped him up too. Moments later Gerald boarded the train in time for his meeting with his parole officer.

Gerald spoke fluidly and with emotion about what he went through in the floods. I have absolute faith that everything written here happened, though in some cases the sequences do not match up with the Katrina timeline. In Gerald's words, *"This is my story, how I remember it, like it happenin' now."*

Susan Orlins

Explanation of Dialect

For the reader to get a true picture of Gerald Anderson, I thought it important for him to tell his story in his own voice. Because he speaks a Southern African-American dialect unique to New Orleans, you will notice many instances of nonstandard grammar as well as unusual spellings meant to communicate his regional pronunciations.

You may also notice that his use of these dialectal features is inconsistent. This may be because of natural variation within Gerald's dialect or because at times he's adjusting his speech unconsciously to bring it more in line with that of the reader, who he may assume speaks standard English.

We thank Charles Carson, managing editor of the journal American Speech, *for his insights about dialect.*

Susan Orlins

WHEN I WAS SIX, I BEGAN TO NOTICE MY brothers' and sisters' daddies come around on Fridays and Saturdays and give them money. I ask my mama, "Where my daddy at?"

She say, "I don't know. He might be in his bird house."

I ask, "What is this bird house?"

She say, "Jail, where he always at."

My mama had eight kids and I had one strong will. We were five boys and three girls with three or four different daddies. I was Mama's second to youngest.

The New Orleans neighborhood I came up in, you can see the ladies, the players, the hustlers, the dogfights, the stolen cars. It be right there. You sit on the porch, and it like watchin' a wrassling match. Some action gonna go on all the time. If there ain't men doin' violence, women be fightin' about card game or about men.

My oldest brother used to say he gonna break my arm if I don't go to school. The more I aware what he gonna do, the more I got in trouble. My brother would pick me up, hold me to the ceiling and drop me. Boom! One hour later I go right back and disobey him.

After a while nothin' hurt you. It like a bee sting, it hurt for a minute and go away.

One day another brother send me out for Ritz crackers and beef jerky. All he say, "Don't pay for it." He tell me the only way he let me go outside is if I don't pay for it. He make me promise not to let Mama know. That's how I got started. I was seven years old.

When I was 15, to get into the clubhouse with my friends you hadda bring food. So I stole sardines. I got caught and got sent to juvenile detention.

In juvie, I learned from other inmates how to smoke weed and snort cocaine, which visitors smuggled to them inside potato chip bags.

Ten years later I met up with my daddy in Louisiana State Penitentiary. He arranged to have me moved to the section where he at.

He said, "Man, let me tell you somethin'. I love you, but I had to do what I had to. I just don't wanna see you die here beside me."

So I know that mean my daddy got a little care about

me. That make me want to stay out. I told him, "We all make mistakes."

I made plenty of mistakes too, but I believe in second chance. I didn't give people time to communicate with me. I was on drugs, and all I could think was one thing: find a way to get high.

Three weeks before Katrina hit, I got released from prison after serving eighteen months for burglary. During the days I went to the projects and hung out with old friends. I was back on the street but staying out of trouble.

Then the rain began, and I heard a broadcast about a big storm comin'. My ears perked up. Whenever there was bad weather on the way, my criminal mind turned to negative thoughts.

While people was talkin' about the hurricane, I was thinkin' how I could go out and do some hustlin'—break into cars, stores, homes. I wasn't hoping for a hurricane, just enough of a pourdown for the power to go off, so I could go out and get things I couldn't afford to buy, like clothes, shoes, and televisions. And, of course, drugs.

When I did crime, I didn't think about gettin' locked up. That like jinx to me. I always expected to get away with it, even though I always got caught. It was the only life I knew.

GERALD ANDERSON

With all the hurricane talk, friends was sayin' things like, "You got the whole of New Orleans in your pocket."

But it got dangerous, and I had to think how to survive. For that, I be glad I got some skills I learned in prison.

2

I WAS THIRTY-SEVEN YEARS OLD AND LIVED WITH MY mother, sister, three nephews and a pit bull named Spot, who had a ring around his eye, like Pete in "The Little Rascals." One morning after the weatherman say the hurricane about to hit, the mayor come on TV offering places to go: schools, churches, the Superdome.

Mama worried somethin' gonna happen to the three-bedroom home our family been livin' in for thirty years, a two-story house on Jackson, a street that run four blocks straight to the river.

Mostly, though, Mama worried 'bout what the weatherman say. She tell us "Get your clothes and whatever else you need. We leaving."

I was like, "I'll help y'all, but this storm ain't gonna be." It took all day for me and my friends to move my family and Spot—with their clothing, cosmetics, and dog food—one mile away to the Superdome.

The whole time it was pouring and thundering. I never felt rain like this, so hard it knock you down. Under my raincoat, my T-shirt so wet it stick to my chest. My feet soaked through my Nikes. And my skin all over feel gritty from dust, sticks, and trash flyin' around.

But still, it was like the floods I remembered from when I was a kid that I would go out and splash in.

After hauling the last load to the Superdome, me and my friends went back to the house. It had a whole different vibe now, a haunted house vibe. Maybe the loud, steady *whoosh* makin' it spooky, like a angry beast right there with us in the living room.

We decided to walk to the projects, which was on higher ground, just a few blocks away. Outside you could feel the whole earth vibrating; it smell like the bottom of a incinerator.

When we got to the projects, my friend there say, "The power's out."

I told him, "Man, don't worry about that. Power always goin' out."

Suddenly we hear, BOOM! We come to learn the water be out too.

Wires on the ground look like scribble scratch. Service trucks parked up and down the block, while utility workers be up on poles, tryin' to repair power lines. The whole time rain keep pounding away.

That night, we eating tuna fish out of cans to the sounds of supermarket carts rattlin' on the street. People had went to different markets to get baskets, so they could push they belongings to the Superdome.

I fell asleep hearing branches hittin' houses, roof shingles crashin' to the ground, and cracking sound of big ol' trees fallin' so loud you think they about to bust your eardrums. The whole time, the whooshing never stop.

Even though I was saying it's a joke, all that fuss about the hurricane, part of my mind was tellin' me there could be somethin' happening. I was kinda at peace with it, because I knew my family be safe. I was like "Lord, whatever you do, keep my family safe. And everyone else's family too."

And then things got really bad.

E VEN IN DAYTIME, THE SKY BE DARK LIKE NIGHT.
I woke up at the projects hearing cries in the distance. From the balcony, I could see the interstate—with so many cars, it look like the Saints just made it to the Superbowl.

All day below us, families was streamin' on foot to the Superdome, kids on they daddies' backs, because now the water be over the head of them little ones. Babies was bawlin' and the water level kept rising.

I yelled down, "Where y'all goin'?"

A woman around my mama's age called back, "Y'all better get out of the projects while y'all can." Families that didn't get along before the Katrina were now helping each other.

Seven of us was havin' fun up on the fourth floor, playin' cards and dominoes. We lit candles and put hot dogs from the refrigerator—along with ice that hadn't yet melted—into the cooler. Just knowing those franks be there made us hungry. Soon we grilled them out on the balcony.

Some of the guys started sayin', "I wish I woulda gone with them."

The rest of us razzed, "Now you wanna chicken out. You scared."

Without air conditioning, it was too crazy hot to be indoors a second night, so we dragged sofas, chairs, and pillows onto the balcony, to hang out and also to sleep there. We had plenty of space, because they had no partitions between neighbors.

Although we kinda sheltered by a overhang, rain blowin' sideways drenched us while we slept in the open. I never seen a night black as zebra stripes like that.

In the morning, there still be thunder and windows shatterin' and trees cracking. Us guys got in a huddle and said, "Man, this thing gettin' intense."

"This thing actually comin'."

"Too late to cry about it now."

"We gotta stand up to it," I said, "and face whatever about to happen."

The flooding got so high, like I'd never seen before. I'm nearly six feet tall and if I went down, the water be up to my nose. It seemed crazy to even try, but curiosity was burnin' inside me like a sizzlin' fry pan.

I told the others, "I don't care what y'all say, I'm goin' down." At least I knew how to swim. Some guys didn't. Three friends followed me.

Wearing shorts, a basketball jersey, and sandals, I began to half swim, half wade through the flooded streets.

Tin roofs was getting blown off houses. Trash was blocking drains, so rainwater be backing up and streets be flowing like the Mississippi.

We saw families prayin', people wailin' and hollerin', "I want to get away." Helicopters buzzed overhead. To get their attention, folks was waving white rags.

We made our way over to the Garden District, the rich folks' side of town, where a boat sat in the driveway of a evacuated house. That house look fine as a daisy, painted all yellow with white shutters. Inside the garage we found some plywood that we took to use for paddles. We also took rain jackets, boots, goggles, and flippers that was hanging on racks in the back. We put on the jackets and tossed the rest into the boat and then climbed in.

We floated down the street, waving at some folks who was in big boats like ours. Others was travelin' on jet skis. When the current didn't carry us, we paddled with the plywood sticks. I called out, "Anyone want a ride to the Superdome?"

I felt almost festive, cruisin' past what—only days earlier—had been them proud-looking houses painted in pink, yellow, and blue colors with tidy lawns and big ol' porches. Little did we know what was waitin' for us on our way back to the projects.

4

W E PADDLED BACK TOWARD THE PROJECTS WITH the wind whipping like it furious about somethin'. A guy standin' on a porch and wildly waving his arms called out, "Man, I need help."

I asked my friend, KK, "Who's he?"

"His name's Calio," KK said. "He moved here while you were in jail."

KK pointed to me and yelled back to Calio, "He's the dude I told you about who was locked up."

I hollered to Calio, "What you need help with?"

He said, "Michelle back in our house. She wouldn't go to the Superdome without me and I didn't want to leave."

"So what?" I said.

And then he answered, "She my baby mama and she real pregnant. She in pain and now the water too high.

She can't get outta the house. We gotta find a way to get her out."

Michelle was in their place a few doors over. Calio come to this porch to get help, because it on higher ground.

Calio climbed into our boat and we paddled to the house to help Michelle. We pulled close to the steps, so the water level only be up to our chests.

When we opened the front door, a flood gushed in, drenching toys that were scattered about. Michelle's two sons—eight and twelve—was upstairs in a bedroom, while Michelle laid on the sofa screaming, her belly swollen like a big ol' beach ball, her body in spasm with labor pain.

I called up to the kids, "You all right?"

They yelled back, "Yeah, but we scared!"

I told them, "Everything be okay. Just stay up there."

There was too much water to get Michelle out though. So I asked Calio, "I don't know how to deliver a baby, do you?"

He said no, so I told him, "Then we gotta get Michelle outta here! Do you have some tools we can use to break the roof in?" Helicopters was buzzing like a hive of bees in the sky. If we could get on the roof, I figured we could try to flag one down to help us.

Calio said there was tools, but they was out back in the shed.

We ran around lookin' for a way out to the shed.

A door in the kitchen seemed like our best shot, so we opened it and waded through chin-high water. In the shed we found a sledgehammer, crowbar, axe, power drill (though we had no power), and an old twenty-four-foot ladder. We grabbed all that stuff and held it over our heads, pushing against waves to get back to the house.

The second we got everything inside, we set up the ladder in the middle of the living room.

Then I asked, "Who gonna get up there first?" We just looked at each other. We were all big guys, weighing around 240 pounds, except Calio—he was a slim, little guy.

No one spoke up, so I said, "I'll get up there." I headed up the ladder with a long crowbar in my hand, and then I took a whack at the ceiling. A chunk the size of a toaster crashed to the floor. I felt like I was about to break an Olympic record for bangin' a roof in.

The whole time Michelle thrashin' and hollerin', "Help me! Get me outta here!" The more she hollered, the more it made me move my body. It like her cries be wild dance music instead of screams of a woman in childbirth pain. I banged harder and harder.

Us guys kept taking turns beatin' at that ceiling. It seemed like hours.

With all our hammerin' noise, Michelle cryin', and the helicopters whirrin', it give me the creeps how quiet the kids was. I worried how they be doin', but didn't want to set them off by askin'. We had to keep pounding away.

Finally we broke through to a sliver of sky the color of prison rats. We kept taking turns up the ladder, while two of us held it below. We threw down dry wall, plywood, insulation, and roof tiles. The hole grew bigger and bigger, large enough for Calio to climb to the top of the ladder, poke his head and arms through, and wave a white sheet. We held the ladder as tight as we could, as if by squeezing it, we could make Michelle wailin' stop. And make help come sooner.

5

WHILE MICHELLE DOIN' HER AGONY ON THE sofa, and Calio tryin' to wave a helicopter outta the sky, the military be dropping boxes with food and water. The supplies fell with big splashes and then floated on the floodwater. Inside the boxes we found hot meals of Salisbury steak, peas, mashed potatoes, meatballs and spaghetti and Snickers.

I took some food upstairs to Michelle's two boys. They huddled together lookin' all wide-eyed on the bed they shared.

They ask me, "What's happenin'?"

"The water gonna come in here?"

"Mama gonna be okay?"

I assured them, "Mama be fine. Soon y'all have a new baby." Like us all do, they relieved themselves in a bucket, which I emptied into a plastic bag and took downstairs.

After about forty minutes of Calio up the ladder and us wonderin' whether help would ever come, we heard the whirring get louder and louder. And then we hear Calio shouting to someone.

I yelled up, "Calio, who you talkin' to?"

He called down that a helicopter seen him, and I was like, "For real?"

He say, "Yeah!"

"Tell them to come quick!"

The helicopter *brrrrrm brrrrrm* got closer. It feel like it motorizin' the whole house.

Calio come flyin' down the ladder, breathin' all heavy, "The helicopter man say move our ladder! Quick! They gonna get in here! Now!"

I grabbed our ladder away just in time for the guy steppin' down a wiggly ladder that attached to the helicopter.

Three more guys came down. One asked, "Man, why didn't she leave?" But he didn't wait for an answer.

He rush over to Michelle and tell her to stay calm, open her legs, and breathe. She screamin' and cryin' and rockin' her head back and forth.

I could hardly watch and ran into the kitchen. But then I peeked out, just in time to see a slimy, bitty infant oozing out between her legs. A medic stroked the little body, and a squeaky *whaaa whaaa* came from its tiny mouth.

It's hard to say—was it an hour later? Two hours later? They put the baby in a sack—like a duffle bag— and hauled him up the ladder and through the roof. One guy wrapped Michelle in a big ol' sling and towed her up next to be with her new son and escape the nightmare we was facin' down below.

They already took Michelle's other two boys up in sacks, and they offered to take the rest of us. But I insisted, "No can do buddy."

The helicopter man asked Calio, "You sure you don't want to come?"

He answered, "I'm gonna stay. I know you gonna look after my family."

I *still* wasn't believing it. I couldn't imagine this getting any more extreme, even though the helicopter man say, "I don't know why y'all staying here. It's gettin' worse. It's sitting in the gulf—ten hours from now it's gonna hit. I'm telling y'all, get outta here!"

I told him, "If it do hit, I know how to survive it. I'm not leavin' my hometown." I thought I was a smarty.

By the time I realized I should have listened, it was too late.

I SAID TO MY BOYS, "I'M TELLIN' YA, MAN, WE SHOULDA gone on that helicopter. Y'all shoulda followed your own minds. Let's get back to the projects and higher ground, where everyone at."

Outside, the water still up to our nose. Toppled trees and tangled wires be impossible to paddle through, so we pushed the boat. Was it only one day ago that these floods startin' to really bully us?

We passed cars that be completely underwater, lookin' like big ol' whales. Others was floating. One family got stuck tryin' to get to the Superdome in a Brown's Velvet Dairy truck.

I pointed to cats meowing on a high ledge and shouted, "They got more sense than we got!"

Along the way, we met a man whose roof was bust in. He told us they was sleepin' in the bathtub. Another family on they porch huddled like they the New Orleans Saints but, truly, they huddled in prayer. I prayed too, with every move I made.

Alongside our boat, dogs was trying to get help, just like all the humans. Some had the mange with scabs and patches of missing fur. They paws spinnin' like pinwheels, fightin' the currents for they lives. On top of the water, bloated, lifeless bodies of little bitty puppies rushin' past.

Another thing make this like a nightmare, but one where you awake, was all the signs scrawled on houses: *Please help us! People Dog Cat . . . Need food! . . . GRANDMA INSIDE NEED DIALYSIS! . . . Bush get down here right now!*

People trapped in they homes screamin'. That's when I began thinkin' 'bout the inmates I left behind when I got released from Orleans Parish Prison a few weeks before. What if I still be locked up?

And with this thing gettin' rougher by the minute, I didn't wanna imagine what guys was goin' through in "the hole," an underground cell beside the morgue where unruly inmates got sent for fighting or other misbehavior. I knew how it was, 'cause I be put in the hole for smokin' cigarettes.

If you in the hole, you get one scoop of oatmeal twice a day and one sandwich—that's it. And the rats in the hole? They the fattest rats I ever seen. They crawl all over, and they don't run away from you neither.

Bein' below ground, the hole surely be flooded. I wondered about my friend Smiley, who was always gettin' in fights with deputies and other inmates. *He probably trapped in the hole right now,* I thought.

I also wondered about friends in prison I played cards and domino with, and even a few deputies I was cool with. I used to talk to them at night about the street and what I do if I beat the charge. I'd tell them, "I'm never comin' back. I'm gonna find a nice job, get a new life."

They say, "Aw man we heard you tell that story before."

My biggest worry in prison be getting to the dentist or doctor. If you say you got a toothache, they tell you, "Go lie down." It might be days before you see the nurse or doctor. Some guys need dialysis a few times a week. We had a separate unit for inmates with AIDS.

I be under a lot of stress in prison, but I had to stand strong to make it. It like going to war; you can't put your head down or you'll lose the battle.

But now, I'm afraid that deputies be goin' home to they families. What would happen to the inmates behind bars? It wasn't until after Katrina that I read about deputies abandoning prisoners without food or drinking water. I heard that some inmates—bein' criminal-minded—filed down toothbrushes and bush combs to make them into keys, which they used to pop locks. Some escaped, some stayed behind to help others.

There was nothin' anyone could do to rescue those behind steel doors—the guys in solitary. Some inmates, who suffered from conditions like diabetes and epilepsy, didn't have their medication. Some prisoners never made it out.

Many of the prisoners left to fend for theyselves—without food or drink in the rising sewage waters—were teenagers; and many of them held for minor violations; some never even been charged.

As for me, my time in prison was sweet like Mama's pecan pie compared to this battle with the floods.

7

ON THE WAY BACK TO THE PROJECTS, ME AND my homies moved five bodies—two ladies and three men—out of the water and put them on dry ground. We did this out of respect, but also because the wet, decaying corpses was making the neighborhood stink. One guy—he a white guy, a taxi driver—was purple and his body hard to the touch, but he so blown up it look like you could take a needle and pop him.

When we finally got back to the projects, we let every family know that in less than ten hours Katrina would hit. We told them what the helicopter rescuers told us, "When it hits, crouch down on the floor." I wondered whether this was how it felt inside a airplane that about to crash.

A hollow sound of flooding got deeper, like a echo that never stops. It was August and, if this flood not happenin', I be wet, but with sweat. The way the wind blow the rain now, it chill my bones worse than if I be locked in a meat freezer.

We distributed a whole stack of food boxes that we collected in the boat to families at the projects. I felt like the military, supporting others.

My buddies and me swapped turns sleeping; someone always stay awake to watch that everybody okay. If one of us said, "Let me catch a nap," another said, "Get some rest. I ain't goin' nowhere."

Some younger kids tried to put on brave faces, but I could see fear in they eyes. To keep them from goin' down to play in the water, we blocked the stairways on both ends of the balcony, which was as long as a football field.

Calio asked us, "You scared? Watcha think gonna happen?"

I said, "If you scared, you shoulda gone with the helicopter guys who took Michelle and her baby. Y'all shoulda thought about goin' to church all these years."

People say there's not a God, but someone had to be lookin' after us. We was like one huge family on this big ol' balcony. I led prayers for all the men, womens, children, and even puppy dogs. "Lord we come together today to remove this thing that we are facing. Not just for us but for everyone else that's facing this terrible thing they say gonna happen. God always say two or more gathered together, he's in the midst. There be people in the hospital, people who can't walk, people who can't see. We ask for everyone."

Just then, a friend ran out on the balcony. His mother was having a seizure. From bein' in prison I knew what to do; I had cellies who had seizures. So I ran behind him and when we got to her she was foaming at the mouth.

I turned her on her side, and then I sat on top of her with all my weight, so she couldn't move. After twenty minutes the seizure was over. I helped her to a couch and talk to her, and when she talk back, I know she okay.

Me and my buddies chattin' with everyone, while we took inventory of the residents. "Lillian, where do you think your boys went?" I asked an old woman.

"Last time I seen them they was going to the Superdome," she said. Like so many others, she had no contact with her sons and was fretting.

Another neighbor kept askin', "Where my grand-baby at?"

By now my group of friends was up to about two dozen, most of us in our thirties. All the way down the balcony, neighbors bunched up, talkin' just like it be a family day, like a reunion, which helped keep they minds off all the worry.

Later, I sat thinkin' 'bout whether I was gonna to make it and why I'd talked my friends into staying, just 'cause I didn't wanna leave my city. If I heard the weatherman say that now, I wouldn't wait to find out what about to happen. I'd be in the next state.

My guilt motivate me to step forward and do whatever it took to help others.

That night, under sky that look like it smeared with tar, I slept on one of the sofas we dragged out to the balcony. By morning, rain comin' down so hard, it sound like ice.

8

I CAME AWAKE IN THE EARLY MORNING OF AUGUST 29. At first everything be nice and quiet, so quiet you know somethin' about to happen. And then thunder and big, big lightning strike. BOOM! CRACK! Wind blowing, windows shakin', like you never thought you'd see.

I ran floor to floor in the projects, telling people, "Get down! Get down and pray!"

Some folks was nervous, some screamin', "We ain't gonna make it!"

I said, "We gonna make it. Just stay down! You gotta use the bathroom? Well, you can't move!"

Layin' flat out, face down for hours . . . honestly, it hard to do.

We stayed face down till daylight. Well, it became daytime, but not exactly light. You could come up but you couldn't go out. We was on the balcony, scared.

The wind was speeding like a race car. And spinning. You ever seen rain spin?

Cars, vans, and families with trailers on the interstate were all jammed up, not moving. After a while, I saw other people starting to move, and I wanted to go out too, see what was goin' on.

I told my friends, "I want to go out right now. We got nothing to lose. We got a boat, we got some strong gentlemans, we oughta go now!"

They said they was tired, and I couldn't move the boat by myself. But when something happens, you're gonna push your body—and your buddies—to do it. I had faith I could find a way for us to win the fight against the floodwater and get supplies.

All my talk made a lotta folks in the projects stay put, rather than evacuate, and now I had to make a way to get everything they needed. Finally, I got a few guys to come with me.

When we got downtown, the water was much worse than it was uptown by the projects. Sewers were blocked up and waves was spilling over the sides of the boat.

My buddies was scared. They didn't know what they'd find in the flooding. A few weeks earlier, there was a big ol' snake in the neighborhood. Now, my homeboys afraid there be snakes or gators in that nasty water.

There could also be giant nutra rats that look like armadillos. To me, those nutra rats looked human. If you threw something at them, they wouldn't move!

But I wasn't scared. Only thing scare me be frogs—they look at you with them bulgy eyes and go ribit. One time my friends put a frog on my shoulder and thought it hilarious when I squealed and ran away, all 240 pounds of me.

We didn't come upon life that day, though, only death: puffed up bodies of people and their pets.

We went back to the projects, hoping it would be easier to get supplies tomorrow.

9

ME AND THREE OF MY HOMEBOYS WOKE UP AND headed out in the boat to look for families that needed help.

We paddled around so many fallen trees, it was like you in a jungle. You heard water all around, going *wooo, wooo,* but you don't hear nothin' usual, no music, no nothin'.

Remember, Katrina happened in August. That seafood time. Ordinarily, you be hearing rap, having block parties, deejays. We have seafood night, and somebody might pay for a jazz band to come play in the projects.

People be partyin', kids running in the playground. Folks throwin' horseshoes, *kling kling.* Playin' basketball, *boom, boom.* Throwin' frisbees. Some people trainin' their pitbulls to fight. You would smell gumbo, jambalaya, fried fish, fried chicken, and yaka mein, which is a kind of soup with noodles, meat, chopped-up onion.

People selling dinners, like fish plate with stuffed crab, cabbage, bean and rice.

Residents from the projects go to the seafood market or go fishing in Lake Pontchartrain and catch catfish, perch, crabs. And then they clean them and sell what they catch.

But now you could hear a mouse pee on cotton. That's how silent it feel, because of missin' all them sounds. It would be a day like you sometimes want . . . quiet and peace, but not the way it was goin' down now.

Me and my homeboys tried to row past the Superdome, but a guard stop us and say, "If you come this way, you gotta go into the Superdome and stay."

So we turned the boat around and headed down Poydras Street, toward the river. Some families be sitting out and we gave them food boxes that military helicopters dropped. We was on a mission to help. But we also wanted to be nosy, to see what goin' on.

When we heard sharp crackling and splashing sounds, we paddled toward them. Around a bend, police officers was throwing bricks at store windows with glass shattering all over the place. Other cops carryin' TV's, computers, and clothes out of a store. It was the kind of store that had everything, bigger than Walgreens but smaller than Walmart.

Seein' the cops loot was like a license to join in. We waited until they left and then lined up to pass things out to each other. I went in the store and filled my arms with whatever folks back at the projects might need: jackets, jeans, socks, blankets, candles, batteries, flashlights, charcoal, tuna, and sardines. I passed armfuls to Calio, who was standing by the broken window. He then passed the stuff on down until KK put it all in the boat.

Paddlin' back to the projects, we come up on a Chicken in the Box with a broken window. I jumped out of the boat, and climbed through the window to get a matchbook. Calio say, "Man, you gonna smoke a cigarette? You smell like a thousand pounds of gas! You gonna blow yourself up!"

From being in the floodwater, a layer of gasoline coated my body, so I thought twice before lighting one of the cigarettes that I kept zipped in a plastic baggie. But I was dyin' for a smoke.

I tell him, "We blow, we blow. Y'all can step over there." But then they all want a cigarette too.

After surviving a smoke and paddling farther down, we see more people breakin' into stores. But the cops get out of they cars and shoot the looters with rubber bullet guns that go bang! You shoulda seen those guys jump; they drop everything and run.

After that, the cops went into the stores and come out pullin' big ol' duffle bags, stuffed with every kind of everything for theyselves.

Finally we made it back to the projects, where the stink of trash and sewage and decaying bodies make me feel like I gonna throw up.

We asked, "Do anyone need batteries, water, dominoes, playing cards? We got it all. We the store now. The free store. Paper plates, napkins, tissue paper. We can go out and get more." We tried to make people feel comfortable, take the chill out their bodies.

Just as everyone enjoying the new stuff, my homeboy KK, who's like a little twenty-seven-year-old brother to me, come up the steps bawlin' his eyes out, and I say, "Man, what's wrong?"

He run up gaggin' and gaspin' and cryin', "Y'all hear about my grandma and my little cousins?

10

MY HOMEBOY KK, KEEP CRYIN' AND REPEATIN', "Y'all hear 'bout my grandma and my little cousins?"

KK's grandma was Miss Mary. I used to clean her yard. She like a grandma to all of us. She'd cook us mustard greens and pig tails and cornbread. On Fridays, she'd make fish plate and fried chicken. Her cookin' make you say, "Mmmm."

Miss Mary always have a family day at the park with so much food you could bring a doggie bag home. It was a good family, a party family.

But now KK say, "We went to check on our grandma and our little cousins. My grandma and my family dead. Someone come in the house and kill them."

KK say they get there and see Miss Mary and the kids shot up and stabbed up, house all bloody, the beds, the kids' rooms, everything. And KK saw the safe. It was open and empty. I thought, *It had to be someone who knew she had a safe.*

As soon as we heard that, we started bringing all the kids in the projects more close to us. The kids was scared and we was scared. We knew we had to watch them even more now. Somebody had to stay on post.

Up on that big, long balcony, we was just like if we was protectin' the President's house; someone always on lookout. You come up? We pat you down. We had no metal detector or nothin', but we gotta make sure everything all right.

I put my head down and say, *Lord I'm glad my family's away. For those whose families ain't away, they ought to get away.*

We feel the pain of Miss Mary's family. As I said, the lady was like a mother to us all. We had to go and see what was happenin' in that house.

We didn't go empty-hand. My homeboys put all kind of thing in that boat: bush knives, screwdrivers, hammers, little hand-saw blades. We didn't know if someone still be in the house. We wasn't lookin' for no trouble. We just tryin' to come outta this alive.

A lot of us went over there, like eight of us, including KK and some of his older cousins. We all piled into the boat, which was long like a canal boat. Mind you, the floods was still goin' on with pouring down rain and rattling thunder and wind that feel like an elephant against your chest. People looking lost, desperate.

On the way to Miss Mary and them kids, we passed a house with a sign on the door that said "DEAD BODY INSIDE," but we know only thing that kill that body was the flood.

We paddled a few more minutes and then Miss Mary's little white, wooden house come into view. So far, it look normal.

As we floated nearer, we could see the windows and back door wide open. We pulled up close. That way we could wedge the boat to keep it from drifting and we could climb right onto the porch. But we make sure one of us stay and watch it.

We entered Miss Mary's house and knew not to touch nothin'; we use rags off the boat to touch the front door. The rug was squishy but there wasn't too much flood, because the house sat some steps up off the ground, even though those steps was now washed away.

Inside the house, ain't no power, no electricity, no phone, no police, no nothin'. The first body I seen was Miss Mary stretched on her back on the sofa, wearing one of them grandma dresses. If you know how Miss

Mary be when she call you into the house to have some gumbo or go to the store for her, you think she just layin' on the couch watchin' her daily stories, like "The Young and the Restless," the way she always do. Except now you see blood all down the front of her grandma dress.

It put chills in my body. As good as that lady was, it took everything outta me to see her that way. It was like you wanted to say "Goddamn!" We was all in big shock, lookin' at each other, putting our heads down. *Who gonna do this to her?*

You feel so weak, it feel like you dead. I ain't gonna say every day—but just about every week most of my life—I might be seeing three or four dead bodies that been shot in the project or that somebody found in an abandon building. You see families fighting, stabbing each other. Boyfriend and girlfriend fighting.

So I was used to seein' dead people, but I ain't never seen anyone murdered that open her heart to you like Miss Mary. She meant so much to me.

I knew the grandkids was in they bedrooms, and now I had the hardest thing: to follow KK and see them kids all bloodied up.

11

I WORRIED THE MURDERERS MIGHT STILL BE IN THE house. So five of us stayed close and tipped upstairs, quiet as we could, holding each other by shirts. I was scared and stayed in the middle of the line.

After we went step-by-step, KK led us to the room where the four kids was, three boys and one girl, ages nine, eleven, thirteen, and fourteen.

It was a horrible sight, them children stabbed up like that. Why you gonna kill these kids? Whoever did it knew the kids, because they must be afraid the kids know their faces. That's how it registered me. The kids didn't do you nothin'; the lady didn't do you nothin'.

We could see the stab hole in the clothes and blood splattered everywhere. It had to be more than one person who entered the house and done that terrible thing.

Two kids on the bed, one layin' on the floor by the closet, one by the TV, spread out like . . . y'know . . . there was no mercy. All I could do is bend my head and say *Lord*.

Now we gotta stay more focus.

After leaving poor Miss Mary and her grandkids all bloody in that sweet house I used to go to, now like a horror house, we paddled toward the Ninth Ward, a low class downtown neighborhood.

Nearly every house had signs like "Help! Need food!" We about to stop and pass out meals the helicopters dropped when we saw a family in an old wooden shack with wind screens hanging and broken windows and the stairs washed away. They had no way to get out.

I said, "Stop the boat." We paddled up to where the steps had been and I stood— balancing in the boat— and knocked on the door. They open the door but they really scared at first. They ask who we was.

And I'm like, "We ain't troops or nothing. We just helpin' out."

The lady like, "Oh y'all out there just helpin' people?"

The kids in the house, they so happy to see someone come. They too was like, "Who is y'all?"

One kid say, "You see all that water comin' in there? Can you help us get outta here?"

I'm like, "We can help you get outta here but we gotta bring you to the Superdome."

He say, "Anywhere but bein' inside here, because we don't look like we gonna make it." He around eleven years old, but he talk grown, like grown talk.

After we done takin' the people to the Superdome, we pass a National Guard truck with K-9 dogs and officers wearing orange vests. Some of them be in a motorboat.

They ask, "Where y'all goin'? What y'all doin'?"

I say, "We just helpin' families much as we could. We ain't doin' no crime, sir. We ain't tryin' to do no violence or nothin'. We helpin' escort families to the Superdome."

They say, "Y'all see any other families around here?" I tell them they got people all in the projects and in they regular houses too.

One guard ask me, "You ever been in the military?"

I say, "No, but I been a junior lifeguard comin' up."

He tell me this water gonna be gettin' more higher till we all under the water. He say, "If ya need anything just look for the orange vests." He also mention a lot of robberin' goin' on and people getting' robbed up on the interstate by gunpoint.

And then he ask, "You sure y'ain't got no weapons, no guns or nothin'?"

"Well," I say, "I be honest with you. We ain't got no guns, but we got screwdrivers and hammers, because we just left a house with Miss Mary, a fine lady that like a grandma to us, and she got shot dead in her house."

He say, "Can y'all show where that house at? That's the kind of thing we looking for."

I tell him yes sir and he say, "We gonna follow behind y'all." They follow us in their motorboat.

We get to the house and they say, "Y'all know anyone ya think mighta did this here?"

I say, "No sir. Honestly? If we'd a seen faces, y'all ain't got a chance to bring them to jail 'cause my homeboys woulda finished them off."

After he say we can leave, we go back to the projects. Upstairs a grandma come running to tell us her little grandson gone missing.

12

WHEN THE GRANDMA TELL ME THE LITTLE BOY went missing, I say to myself, *Lord don't tell me the killing got close to us now.*

I asked, "When the last time y'all seen him?"

She say, "He was out earlier playing with the other kids on the balcony. He looked like he was mad or ain't feel good or somethin."

First thing that come to my mind was to tell KK, Calio, and the others to spread out and go floor to floor lookin' for this boy. His grandma say he four years old.

We start searching, but the projects be one big building, like fourteen apartments on each floor. And there be four floors.

I asked the other kids, "Where y'all last playin' at?"

You know how kids are—they just say, "We went up and down, up and down."

As we was searching, we kept responding to each other with our walkie talkies. When I got down on the third floor, I heard mine go *didididididi.*

So I say into my talkie, "What's up?"

Calio say, "Come up to the fourth floor right quick! Hurry up!" So we all run up to the fourth floor.

We entered the apartment Calio was in. He say, "Open that closet right there."

So we open the closet and we see the kid. He wrapped in a quilt blanket and not moving.

I say to myself, *Lord, please please don't let he be dead.*

We didn't see no blood and then Calio say, "He breathing." We still didn't know if this was the kid they talkin' about.

God knows, I'm thinkin', *Please let this be the right kid.*

So Calio went down to the third floor to get the family that say they little boy was missing.

The grandmother and the mother came running so fast. Everyone already knew about poor Miss Mary and her grandkids bein' murdered and all. We all like we balancing on a long, sharp edge.

After the family come in, we showed them the kid in the closet and we moved aside. You shoulda seen the expression on them all face. The first thing out the grandma mouth, "Thank you Jesus."

And then she told us, "He had said he was tired."

The feeling of this family really touch me. I'm so thankful this kid all right.

After that, things calmed down. But not for long.

13

WITH SO MANY FRIGHTS, EVERYONE ON HIGH alert. Before I even knew this day would bring another tragedy, I told my homies, "We gotta make everyone safer. We gotta go out and get more whistles, batteries, and walkie talkies."

Remember, the projects is a four-floor building; we needed to be strategic. I said, "We need a safety plan, so people be safe on all floors at all times. From now on, we gonna equip every family with whistles and those little string things you pull that go *wibiti*, *wibiti* and any other kind of security thing we can find."

We went to each floor and called a meeting with the families on that floor, letting everyone know that every forty-five minutes, we gonna do a head count. We want people to stay put while we count. That way we can keep track of where folks at.

We'll be able to say, hey you seen Kevin? And someone will say he downstairs playin' cards or domino and we know he okay.

We not in prison, but that's how they kept up with us there. You can use things you learn in prison and take them to another level.

So Calio and a friend went out lookin' for more whistles, batteries, and walkie talkies.

Thirty minutes later, Calio hit me on my walkie talkie. I respond quick, even though I be dozing off.

I'm like "Wassup?"

He responded, "Third, can you hear me good?" He called me "Third Ward," because I was so well known in the Third Ward, my uptown part of the hood.

I say, "Yeah man. What's good?"

He panting like a pit bull in a fight and talkin' real fast. He tell me, "I stop by my grandma, because folks say my cousin Tiffany hangin' out on a balcony near my grandma earlier today. I went there lookin' for her.

"Outside in the backyard, the lady next door say she seen Tiffany an hour ago on the balcony. But I don't see Tiffany.

"So I go inside my grandma house. You wouldn't believe me, man, what happened. My cousin Tiffany right there dead! Cut up! dead!"

Calio cryin' and breathin' all heavy, say, "It's time to go to war."

Anything move, look dangerous, he ready to rock it to sleep, but I'm like, "Man, I feel broken-heart about this, but I not playin' with no guns."

He say, "They rock Miss Mary family to sleep. They just rock my cousin to sleep. You know they gotta have one of us on the list."

I tell him, "Man I can't play with no guns."

He say, "Who gonna catch you?"

I say, "Y'all can do what you wanna do, but when it comes to guns, leave me out."

I tell him to come get me. I can't do nothin', but I wanna see it. When he come, we hug each other and I tell him it gonna be all right.

We paddle to see Tiffany. I can't believe it be her with flies feeding on her blood and her body stinking like garbage that been out for a week in summer. Or maybe just everything be smellin' like that.

Even though she dead, I wanna let her know somethin'. I whisper, *I told you, Tiff, what you done in the dark, it come to the light.*

I already know Tiff be slashed up like this one day in her grandma laundry room or somewhere.

14

CALIO COUSIN TIFFANY WAS TWENTY-SEVEN. SHE dressed nice and was real good-lookin'. She a hood girl. That mean she hung out with high-class drug dealers. And every time you look around and one of them get killed in the project, you find out Tiffany just been with them. She make men so jealous they kill each other. Now someone kill her.

We always knew it gonna happen. I know that now she'd be sayin', *I wish I woulda listened.*

I used to tell her, "The hood love you baby. You the model in the hood. You the hottest girl in the hood."

But she was playin' some cutthroat games, like leading guys on. I knew her, I knew her scam. She'd get high and smoke weed and do drugs. She'd make the average man leave his wife, if he don't know her game.

She bring men from other wards in the hood. Ward Three dealers feel she threaten their territory. She be in the club dancing. She dance good. She been stripping. She got a lotta tattoo.

If I say, hey this guy wannna see you dance, she say, "He got money?" It gotta be over a hundred dollars. She a gamer. She lead men on.

Seeing Tiffany's slaughtered body brought memory to me of when I seen Miss Mary and her family—KK's grandma and cousins—soaked in they own blood. Now, me and Calio and KK look at each other and just shake our head.

I seen the look in the eye and I feel the pain of them. Those eyes was sayin' to me, *Third Ward, we can't let this go down like that.*

And I told them, "Man, I feel what y'all sayin' but right now we got 306 people in the projects. We gotta find a way to get everyone outta here. Man, it gonna be all right." Calio and KK both had they head down, listenin' to what I'm sayin'."

Back at the projects, we went up to the fourth floor. After that we walk down the balcony, door to door, talkin' to all the families, askin' them if they all right.

When Calio knocked on Miss Ruby apartment, she open up her door. Inside was her, her grandkids, and her husband. The three-year-old grandson know us so good. He run to the door with a whole lotta peanut butter on his face and ask Calio, "You want some?"

Calio, still hurtin' so bad from seein' him cousin Tiff all sliced up, look back at the boy and laugh and say, "No little man, I'm good. Thanks little man, I needed that smile you give me, little man." I never seen Calio smile the way he smile at that kid, all thirty-two teeth showin'.

That's when I knew he was comin' over a bit what happen to his cousin Tiffany. But deep down I knew the hurt still there.

The boy handed the peanut butter jar out to all three of us. "Who want some?" he ask. I looked at the little kid and say, "Man, when I was a little kid I used to eat that same kind of peanut butter, Jiffrey, with the jelly swirled in."

After that, me and Calio and KK talkin' and I say once again, "We gotta figure a way to get folks outta here."

We each went to different floors, checkin' to make sure everyone be eatin' and feelin' okay and then we radio each other and say, "Radio check," which means everybody good. That don't mean the violence be over.

15

IT STILL RAINING, NOT AS HARD AS IT WAS, BUT IT still raining and the wind blowing and daytime still lookin' like nighttime. Still no power, still no shower, so we go out and get some buckets of rainwater to wash up. That's how we bath. The fire hydrants on too. Must be some baby kids turn them on.

We had bottled water from the helicopters and from the stores with broken windows. In the morning we always keep clean water around—you could dip your cup in there and brush your teeth. Any extra water you wet your towel to wash your face.

We had some fun times in between so much bad. I have my boxers on and go out in the rain with Coast or Ivory soap bars and a clean, big towel. You suds yourself up real good and then rinse off by the fire hydrant.

Afterwards we take the towel and wash it in the bucket, latherin' it up, rinsing it, wringing it out, and hangin' it to dry on them kind of windows you crank open.

We used the same buckets to flush the commode.

One morning I was splashing Calio and he say, "Man that water gonna take you away." Calio a little guy, so maybe it would take *him* away. But I know how to swim; he say he can swim too, but I ain't never seen it.

I was telling some families I could sure use some jambalaya right now or a big ol' pot of gumbo. We appreciate the food the military be droppin' but it nothin' like Louisiana food we used to: turkey necks, pig feet, ham hocks with rice and red bean, mustard green, cabbage, every kind of seafood, and my favorite—fried chicken.

We all lay low till the next day, when we woke up to a lotta shootin'. We was on the new side of the project and the shootin' was on the old side. It sounded like wartime in Saudi Arabia. They was firin' automatic guns. Some people that was out in the water told us there was like twenty boys shootin' at the National Guard, who told them on a megaphone to surrender the guns or they was comin' up to get 'em theyself. The National Guards had shields, stun guns, and bulletproof vests. That's what really make me get shake up.

'Cause remember we got families sleepin' on the balconies. A bullet can come from anywhere and get someone. I know too many folks who dead from stray bullets.

16

I CALLED CALIO ON THE RADIO AND SAID, "HOW WE gonna get these folks outta here?"

But deep in my mind, I was thinkin', *I still want to do more traveling through my hometown to see who else need help.*

So I told Calio we was goin' out again and to call KK, because I wanted another friend with us in the boat. We left some guys on standby at the projects to look over everyone, to make sure everyone be okay while we out. All the while, people sayin' what a hypocrite Bush was.

In the projects they have more men than women, so we counting on the men to take care of the women. We had some strong women helping too. They want to make sure they babies be safe.

So me, Calio, and KK paddle down Saint Charles Avenue—past where the rich folks live—to Canal Street and the poorer area.

The water kind of low down there, so we left the boat to go check out Seventh Ward, where my and KK's cousins and friends and aunts live. They all in between middle class and poor. Farther down from that is where some wind can blow away the houses, they so poor.

The water start comin' up on us. That's when I found out Calio and KK could swim. Not good like me, but they made it to this really high porch to go stand on. There was no place else to go and big waves was comin' at us from a motorboat.

So we all huddlin' together on this little bitty porch, and a man pass near us in his motorboat—the kind like you go out on the lake with. We all scared and hollerin'. KK took off his wet t-shirt and flagged the man down.

The man invite us onto the boat. He had two sets of families with kids under blankets. I begin to think maybe he kidnap the people, 'cause a whole lotta crime takin' place.

He ask, "Where you from? Where you heading?"

I told him we from uptown and we tryin' to go downtown to help folks. Come to find out the guy truly helping people too.

He asked, "Y'all want to stay with me and try to get some families outta here? Something the government oughta be doin.'"

We say, "Sure."

After we ridin' around awhile, the man got to this big ol' hotel where people was hangin' out the window. A few National Guards around there give us water and food to hand out.

There was floods over the roofs of the houses and the water hittin' the motorboat's windshield real hard now. People all up in they chimneys, cryin', holdin' signs. The houses leanin' in the water. The farther down we go the more damage we see.

The old man driving the boat say, "I can't go this way because that's where the levee is, the one they say bust open with all this water."

Meanwhile helicopters are all up *brrrm brrrm,* circling above. It not rainin' too much, but the noise we hear below sound like waves be crashin' through tunnels. Deep waves was hitting the boat.

It remind me of "Jaws." That's how the floods was chasin' people. No shark behind them, but with the wind and water, a whole lotta lives was on the line.

We can't get to them folks on the roofs. They sentenced to death up there.

17

THE MOTORBOAT MAN GIVE US LIFESAVERS WITH ropes attached to the boat so we can swim out to help folks and then he able to crank us in. Problem is we can't get to the houses, because them houses, they cavin' in. Trees fallin' over. It ain't nothin' for that weather to pick them things outta the ground. You got telephone poles split too.

When we saw houses we thought we could reach, the man circle his motorboat, like how you go fishing. We then got off the boat wearing our lifesavers and swam to rescue folks.

We always asked for the kids first. We hold babies up in the air toward the sky, like they was a laundry bag, and glide back to the boat with them. Bigger kids we put on our shoulders.

For grownups, two of us would carry them. My head barely above water.

There was this old man, he ain't got no legs, just his torso. So me and KK carry him. He so scared. He keep sayin', "Please don't drop me. Please don't drop me." Finally we get close enough to pass him over to Calio and the man driving the boat.

That guy with no legs, now he so happy, he say, "Man, thank y'all! Thank y'all!" Another twenty or thirty minutes, his house be gone. He wouldn't've made it. After he safe in the boat, I swam back to get his wheelchair.

We rescued three more families after that. No time to stop and think about what a blessing this was. We drop all them at the ramp to the Superdome and then I push the man up in his wheelchair.

The security at the Superdome ask are we going in too. We say no.

He say, "By right, once you up the ramp you gotta go in."

I say, "We been told that, but we been bringin' people here since the hurricane start." Then me and Calio run to the motorboat and the security man didn't run after us.

Motorboat Man drop us back at our boat. He told us, "If there is any kind of way to get to my house, I'd give you some paddles for your boat—better than them sticks y'all been using." He say he'd try to come back, but we never seen him again.

When we get back up to the project, we ask, "Anything going on?" They say some people hit by bullets on the old side of the projects where the shootin' was.

At night, it pitch dark. You can't see what might come at you. You don't know if a building might fall or if live wires down. Or if somebody try to kill you. There ain't no way to call the cops, so I say we'll check early tomorrow morning when we can see better.

In the project it like the old side against the new side. They beef, they don't get along too good. It not a gang, exactly; it like strugglin' for power in the project.

The next day we went building to building. On the old side they had a old addict named Butch. We find him hit by bullets in his leg and on his side. That bullet burnin' him, and he soakin' wet. Him bleedin' and bein' wet make him drip pink all over. He hollerin' "Help me! Help me!"

He tell us he heard some shot. "I try to run," he said. But then the bullets came at him. He was in the middle of shootin' up his drug and he drop his syringe.

I said, "Man, people dyin' out here and you doin' that? That's crazy!"

He gotta live, and we gotta help him.

18

BUTCH GOT THE SHAKES AND HE HOWLIN' WITH the pain. Ain't nothin' we really could do but get him some towels. He bleedin' so bad, we didn't want to touch that, so we reach him some towels and he tie them around his leg.

Only thing Butch really care about was tryin' to get them drugs in him.

Then me, Calio, and KK go out again, because we knew there be folks out there we *could* help.

We see a U-Haul, not a big one, but one of them baby U-Hauls bobbing and tilting-like. You could see it rockin'. So I say, "Damn! See that truck? Look like somebody in there!"

When we open it, we find a lady and a man inside. They say, "Please help us."

I reach my arms out to them, so they can climb out of the U-Haul and onto the boat with us. I asked the man where he trying to go. He say, "Anywhere."

I tell them, "We can take you to the Superdome."

On the way we run into another dead body, a young girl, probably in her twenties, floatin' in them floodwaters. That's when we started seeing kids' shoes, baby shoes, baby clothes, little girl dresses also floating. We didn't know who the body was; it came from nowhere.

All we could do was let it float by.

I said maybe the lady had kids with her because we seen them clothes and shoes, but we had to just keep movin' to get the people where they goin' at.

When we drop the people from the U-Haul at the Superdome, the National Guard told us whenever we ready to surrender to leave they would escort us with trucks and helicopters. Him sayin' "surrender," it like criminal talk, even though we ain't doin' crime.

What he say to us about leavin', though, stood in the back of my mind. I told KK and Calio that tomorrow we gonna go to the Superdome and Convention Center to let the guards know we got a lotta people stuck here at the projects, who afraid to come out. And that we afraid they ain't gonna make it.

We gonna tell them people here stuck with seizures and bad heart. And that we don't have no food and no more water and people complain they need their medicine and our way of helping them just ain't workin' no more.

We gonna tell them all this, like exaggeratin'. That's the only way to get the guards moving fast like we want them to.

Next day, me, KK, and Calio went to the Superdome and the Convention Center and told the guards they need to get to the uptown projects as soon as possible. I told them it's the one near the Greyhound Bus Station.

The man say, "There any wires?"

I say, "No, it's all clear." They say they'll come.

So we return to the projects. Getting out of the boat, I slipped and hit my face in the water. Something bit me and swole my whole face up.

19

S EEIN' MY FACE ALL SWOLLED UP, EVERYONE ASKIN' me what happened. I told them somethin' bit me in the water. I didn't see what it was, it hit so fast.

It didn't slow us down, though. We got right back into the boat and returned to the Superdome to escort the guards, make sure they go to the projects. We go there and found a whole new K-9 squad with dogs.

The squad had a big boat and four big German Shepard dogs on the boat with them. They followed us to the projects. After we got there, one guard askin' questions.

"How many people y'all have here?"

I told him "Four floors, 306 people."

He ask, "How do you know?"

I said, "We keep a count by this walkie talkie, to make sure we ain't missin' anyone."

He say, "It's dangerous for y'all to be here like this. Anything can happen."

He also say, "Not as fast as you think, but I promise we'll get you all out."

I tell him we been movin' bodies out of the water and we been helpin' people with medical problems.

He say don't no one go out for no reason. Because anything can be in that water. He recognize how my face be swole.

They chained up the dogs on the first floor and me, KK, and Calio took the guards to each floor. They ask people, "You all right?"

Some old ladies say we need medical assistance. Some need dialysis machine, some need heart medicine, some need diabetic medicine.

He ask folks, "Who ever flew on a plane or a helicopter?" These be low class people, who never took a plane or left Louisiana before.

So he explained, "Don't be scared. Ain't nothin' gonna happen. The way we tie you up, you'll be safe. It might be twenty-four or seventy-two hours, but we'll get you out of here."

We told one Guard about the shootin' that went on in the project, and he say, "That's why we have dogs." They be like huntin' dogs, huntin' people down, finding bodies.

He stand up on the balcony with us and say to make sure we tell everybody don't be scared because nothin' gonna happen, we gonna be safe gettin' out.

He explained everything good, talkin' to us like we was the military. He say, "We gonna tie a rope around you and clamp it down. Then we hoist folks up to the helicopter." Calio and KK eyes got so big. I felt mine go wide too.

I brought up, "Who gonna go first up in that plane?" Then the three of us got real quiet.

20

THE K-9 GUARDS AND DOGS HEADED OUT IN THEIR boat. An hour later some National Guards arrive and station themselves, one on each floor, to make sure no one leave the project. They say they stayin' on the floor all night to watch us, and they tell us, "You can't go out for no reason."

Knowing a better security watchin' them, the people be feeling more relaxed: mamas swayin' with little bitty babies in they arms, up-age kids riding them big wheel trikes up and down the long balcony, girls playin' with little baby dolls.

We start to feel so comfortable with the guards, and they talk to us about different things. They askin' us, "What made y'all stay? Why didn't y'all leave?"

And we all askin' them where they been sending people to, how many people in the Superdome, how many people they rescue, how did they get 'em out?

We asked where they gonna send us. They say they gonna send us to the convention center. We didn't know yet that we was gonna be leavin' New Orleans.

I told the guard I didn't have no insulin. I'm a diabetic, and I ain't had no medicine ever since I got out of jail three weeks before Katrina hit. It was havin' me feelin' kinda weak. My eyes feelin' blurry too. But I couldn't just stay down.

We had water coming out of the faucets now, but the National Guard told us not to drink it. Folks was usin' it to wash clothes in buckets. Then they hang the clean, wet laundry on open doors to they apartments and on kitchen cabinet doors.

All I wanna do is go out, but I couldn't. It make you more fearful about goin' out when the National Guard tell you "Don't go!"

It make all kind of thoughts come into my mind, like maybe people from overseas be sneakin' in the country to blow us up. The whole thing had us all on tippy toes.

We begin playing cards and domino all day, tryin' to get our minds off feeling trapped. All we can hear is *BRRRR, BRRR.* Helicopters. Bunches of them over our heads, like armies of little spaceships, and you don't know where they going.

The guards be talkin' and laughin' with the kids and with the grownups too. The guards also play domino and cards with me and my homies. They let us know they trapped just like we was trapped, and they make sure to let us know we be all right.

Finally a Red Cross crew came off some boats, like twenty of them, wearing white vests with the little red cross on them. Several medics wore hard hats. They spread out four or five to a floor, and really help us with our medical.

The next morning, after what seemed like months, I woke up and heard birds for the first time since Katrina began. The sky was brighter too. At first I thought I was dreaming.

I got off my cot and looked out over the balcony. Below, as far as I could see, military trucks were lined up, blowin' they horns. *Wonk, Wonk.*

After I wake up good, I hear folks hollerin', "Yeah! Yeah!" with thumbs up. Some was sayin', "About time!" Others was cussin' Bush out.

That's when I told KK, "This must be our ball call, our final day!"

But I misjudged.

.

21

THE MILITARY TRUCKS MOVED SOME PEOPLE TO the Convention Center. I asked when would they come back and get the rest of us.

They said, "Don't worry. It all ain't gonna happen in one day time."

After that I asked the National Guard a lot of questions. How many people they rescued?

"Over five hundred people, worse off than y'all," he said. He told me some stuck on the roof of they house. Some floating in they cars. Some floating in the water.

I asked how many bodies they seen. He say, "Over two hundred bodies," not counting all the ones he didn't see.

He asked me, "What make y'all stay?"

I told him, "Before Katrina hit and the levees broke, I told a lot of people, 'Don't worry; it aint gonna happen; don't believe the newsman.'"

He also wanted to know what we all have done to survive so far. I told him, "We did all we could, getting food, water, supplies. We also rescuing families with the boat."

Funny thing was, he asked have I ever been in the military. I told him no, but I know how to stay alive because I experienced prison. He asked, "What you mean about prison?"

It felt good to open up with him. I told him a lot of riots go off in prison. It might don't be your friends or people you associate with—inmate go against guards, Mexicans against Mexicans or against white or black. It can go all kind of ways.

What I learned from the riots in prison was like if somebody get hurt, I know not to touch your blood. If someone catch a seizure from getting upset, I know how to hold you up till the nurse come.

Sometimes they have a hunger strike in prison. Like at dinner, someone say the food taste bad. Then others say it taste bad. And soon everyone say it taste bad.

A riot breaks out. They start banging on the plates and shouting dirty words about the cook.

Say one of your people is in line and someone cut in, that can start another kind of riot where y'all gotta be fighting. That looks small, that one little thing, but it ain't. Maybe someone had a bad phone talk with his family or girlfriend and then they just stir it up, like "You gonna let him cut you in line?" And everyone get into it.

Or maybe we playin' basketball and it's our time on the court, but another group tries to take the court. Or someone bump you on the court. That can set off a riot. Groups against groups.

I took some of the negative things, but I learn how to hang tough.

In prison you learn so much, like when we don't have no power, you make a bonfire with a bread wrapper wrapped in toilet paper, then you set a pot of water over the fire, holding the pot with a sock so you don't burn your hand.

Or you take a milk carton and burn it to make hot water for cooking soup. You put hair grease or Vaseline on wrapped toilet paper to help things burn slow. We would cook this way in the shower stall. If you want to burn something in your cell, you gotta put a blind up so the guards and the camera can't see you.

You have an iron in the prison rec room for your unit, and you can put a brown paper bag over your cheese sandwich and iron it to grill it.

The only electric thing you have in your cell is a ceiling light. You can get some long wire and make you a

stinger (you gotta know how to do it or you get elec-
trocuted) by running the wire from the light to the
iron handle of a mop bucket, and then tape it down.
If everything set up right, you can bubble up water in
the bucket after five or fifteen minutes. Just don't let the
guards catch you.

You can put beans or hamburger meat in a double
plastic bag and cook them in the hot water or cook hot
dogs or oatmeal or boil a egg or spaghetti.

That night on the project balcony, me and the
National Guard got talking so much, I forgot what was
goin' on all around us.

22

Y'KNOW HOW, WHEN YOU FEEL COMFORTABLE with someone, you can open up?

That's how I felt about the National Guard. He about forty years old, only a few years older than I was, and we kept talkin' real good, sittin' there on the balcony at the projects.

I told him that in prison, I learned how you can use two batteries and a razor blade to start a fire. So with us not having power during Katrina, I would take two batteries and turn one up, one down, tape them down and connect them with any kind of wire—you gotta know how to separate it and put the razor blade on top—but you can make fire this way.

It like a time bomb, it can tick off any time, so you gotta be real careful. (Don't try this at home.)

In prison, riot breaks out while we tryin' to protect each other; if you can help me, you help me. If you have to be on lockdown after a riot break out, you glad prison culture teach you how you cook. Otherwise, you get tired of eating peanut butter sandwiches on lockdown. We think of it as a bad situation, but we help others.

While everyone around us at the projects waitin' impatient to leave, I open up more to the National Guard. I told him I was a junior lifeguard coming up, and I never forget the things they showed me how to rescue folks in the water, so that help me reach out to help a lot of people now.

I said how, as a young boy, I always wanted to be a police officer or a fireman. When I was fourteen or fifteen, I was thinkin' about that. You had officers comin' to school to talk about it.

But then I started doin' time, and I recognize I couldn't really be no police.

I told the guard I was born and raised in New Orleans. He said, "You know a lot about this city."

I told him, "I sure know the ins and out, the bad side and the good side."

That guard really made me feel comfortable. He told me, "I would put my life on the line to save y'all." That's when I know he really tryin' to help us.

He was sharing his life with me. He a white guy, but he talk more like he black. It seem like he seen a lot of pain in his life, same as me.

The way the guard talk, I could tell he been in trouble. He got a lotta tattoo, too. I'm not sayin' people got tattoo mean they been in prison.

He told me he been to prison because he got caught with weed. And then his parents told him if he didn't want to be in prison the rest of his life, he had to finish school and go in the military.

My mother and friends' mothers talked to *me* like that. When they did, I was hearin' it but not hearin' it. My older brother tried, but he was not like a father; he couldn't control me. My grandma, we eye to eye. She like a father-mother—I came up like a grandma boy.

One day in prison they called me to the chaplain office. With me bein' in the prison system, seein' guys bein' called to the chaplain, bein' told that they family members passed, I knew something like that was comin' for me. The chaplain told me to sit down and told me we got a phone call. Your grandma passed. I had helped others stay strong. Now, I just took it.

When I sit with my grandma, we sit on a bed or on the couch. We sit out real good. She would ask me how you doin'? She get anything outta me. We was real deep with each other.

The guard told me they have so many people at the Convention Center that they layin' on the ground, getting medical help. Some afraid to go on the helicopter.

The way he talk about all the people messed up, like how people was cryin' about they family member, not sure they family member make it, there was so much that shook me up, hittin' the bottom of my stomach.

23

I TOLD THE GUARD ABOUT FINDING BUTCH. I TOLD him, "We got a guy on the other side of the building who a dope fiend. He got shot by a rookie bullet." That's how we say stray bullet.

He ask if I'm willing to go with him where Butch at and I say sure. So he got around seven of the fifteen or so National Guards posted to the projects to come with us.

We all piled into the boat to go check on Butch. When we climbed out of the boat, the guards, who already had their knee guards on, were holding shields in one hand. They moved forward slowly with their guns drawn.

It like a SWAT team surrounding me, the way they would if they was telling a bank robber holding hostages to come out of the bank. The only thing different about a bank robber is they tell him to put his hands on his head. This time, they was tryin' to protect me in case there be shootin'.

There was like three of them ahead of me and several others following me up the stairs. They turn the door-knob and push the door open, and we enter the living room and then the bedroom.

Inside the bedroom, Butch, lyin' there by the closet, stinking with death and bloody and he got maggots that look like intestines already feasting on him. The guards rushed over, but I all I could do is stand back, hold my breath, and look.

Then the guards ask me did I see anybody that was shootin'. I say, "No, because we on the other side of the projects. We heard the shots and then next morning we came over and that's when we know Butch be shot. There were a lot of shells on the balcony. We talked to Butch, but he just say there was a shootout."

The National Guard say they were chasing a bunch of young boys that was shootin' about two nights before Butch was shot, but they didn't catch them.

One of the guards wrote some stuff down and said, "We'll get someone to come rescue the body." After that we got back in the boat and headed back to the newer side of the projects.

Once we got back, we went up on the stairs to the third floor. An old lady come up to the guard and say, "Sir, when they comin' back to get more people?"

And before he answer, she tell him, "I'm not tryin' to get on no helicopter—I'm scared of heights. I'd like to be escorted by boat or on a truck."

That's when a lot of people come up and say they scared of heights too. I myself ain't ever been much higher than the fourth floor of the projects.

The guard answered, "We gonna make it as safe as possible for everyone. We'll be back at sunrise to start gettin' y'all." Up till now, we all been worryin' about when will we be gettin' out. Now we know we be gettin' out real soon, and we worry about that, about being taken up on them big ol' helicopters.

24

A T SUNRISE, THE GUARDS COME WITH HELICOPTERS and trucks and boats. I say to myself, *Oh God, the National Guard didn't lie.*

The guard I been talking to—who'd stayed all night watching over us—said, "Some of y'all gonna move today."

They lined people up five by five. It brought a little flag back to me, because it's how they lined us up in prison when things like a fire or a fight broke out.

Sometimes in prison, one of the guys in lockdown might try to commit suicide, popping a socket with the lead from a broken pencil or creating a smoke bomb by wrapping toilet paper around his hand and then makin' it like a ball and lighting it. The prison keep this kind of thing hush up, because they don't want the outside to know they can't control the inmates.

But now in the projects, the guard asked me to help keep count of how many people we were moving.

So I snapped out of those prison memories and rounded up some of the elderly first.

It was hard to get the old folks to listen to us. But some were like one man, who said, "I'll do whatever it takes so I can get my medical situation helped." Many of 'em was on heart pills or need machine.

One old lady passed out on the balcony because she so scared about the helicopter. She weigh over four hundred pounds and was too heavy for the boat. It took eight of us to help her get over to the helicopter.

Before a helicopter go up, they blow a whistle to indicate which helicopter goes next—it mean "Coast clear, I have a full load, and I'm about to roll out."

So one by one, three helicopters—each with forty or fifty folks from the projects—lift off and head to the Convention Center. With all the other helicopters flyin' around, it look like rush hour in the sky.

I was glad to help, but then you get close and feel that motor vibrating *brrrrrm, brrrrrm* under your feet. I was shakin' once I seen how they was pullin' out. My mind went back to the '80s when a plane crashed in Kenner—a suburb of New Orleans—right onto people's houses. I be so nervous. I know it comin' to me next.

25

AFTER THEY TOOK AROUND 120 PROJECTS FOLKS, we smokin' cigarettes, sittin' around talking, and playing cards. The wind was blowin'. Trees still falling and a big ol' telephone pole go down.

I told the guard, "That hurricane is still here! If I wasn't listenin' to y'all, I'd be sneakin' out, the way I'm prone to.

Otherwise it was a pretty quiet day. Next day, same thing. Another 115 took off on helicopters and in boats. We was headin' out—for real!

I overheard the guard sayin' "We down to seventy-one people now." That's when I went to pieces—I was next to go. I try to pump myself up and tell myself, *If they gotta take me by helicopter, I just want outta here.*

I packed a small bag with clothes and shoes I had looted from the store. And soon enough, the guard say,

"Come with me. It time for y'all to be escorted out."

I say, "Who me?"

The guard I been laughin' with tell me, "Man, you afraid to fly to the Convention Center? You still gonna have to fly again to get to the airport. And then to someplace far."

I never been on a plane before. In prison we be escorted in handcuffs and shackles on Greyhound busses and school busses.

The guard tell me again, "It's your turn to roll out on the helicopter."

When I hear that, honestly, my heart went to beatin'.

I was lookin' at everyone else go. Now it was my turn. I'm not afraid of heights, because when I was a kid I used to jump off roofs. We used to take mattresses and wrassle on them and jump off buildings onto them. Sometimes without mattresses.

The helicopter—it was on a hill and they put out a ladder with a long board over it, so we wouldn't slip off and get hurt. It like walkin' the plank, but into the helicopter.

Inside, you stand up the whole time and they clamp a safety belt around your waist. I put a helmet on. After we locked in, they come back and check to make sure you locked in good before the helicopter pull up.

The guard I been talking to say, "You ready buddy?"

I say, "I can't do nothin' but be ready right now." Then the heli pull up in the air, and my stomach drop like it still on the ground.

Helicopter open, no door. Damn! I looked down, but I didn't look too much down. I look side-eyed down. I wanted to see what goin' on.

All you could see was big, hard water waves, crashing into the Queen Boat and all them ferries.

Honestly, I was really worried—maybe we have to jump. The helicopter controls might get stuck or something.

I was more afraid of crashing than of jumping. Remember, I was a lifeguard and there be water everywhere. But you couldn't tell which was the floodwater and which was the river.

Everything in my insides feel like it move, but not as much as when I see what I see fifteen minutes later.

26

A T THE CONVENTION CENTER, THAT'S WHEN YOU really see what people goin' through.

Just like a hospital, there be Red Cross and all kind of medical. Volunteer medics too. There were babies cryin' and veterans evacuated from hospitals with tubes in their bodies. People in neck brace. People lyin' on the ground, some moanin', others screamin' for help.

So many families huddled together. It looked like the world comin' to an end.

It smell worse than the garbage plant. The odor was louder than a skunk. People that know about a skunk, they'll tell you these things.

The people helping say we'll get better medical attention wherever they send us.

There were trailers where they ask all kind of questions. You had to go through that before you leave. They had like fifty gates where you could line up for medical help.

I told them I was a diabetic and had high blood pressure, so they gave me pills and insulin needles.

They ask how many in your family. I tell them, "My family been gone. I'm just with the people from the projects that I been helping."

KK left the projects before me, so I didn't see him. I spent that night outside the convention center in a tent with others that we had helped make it through this. Like twenty of us sleeping in cot beds, using little aluminum lanterns to see.

In every tent we had boxes of food, water, juices, and milk.

It was sort of like, but I wouldn't say exactly like, bein' in prison. Here you got babies cryin' all through the night, people cryin', people prayin', people just wonderin' where they other part of they family at.

I didn't sleep too well that night, because I worried where my family at. Also, a old lady sleeping next to me have a bleeding ulcer and she screaming all night.

She ask me to reach in her bag. All she had was a bottle of Maalox and some pain pills. I try to tell her she be okay, but I really can't imagine the pain of her situation.

I close my eyes and think about all the suffering.

27

ORNING COME, AND THEY GIVE US FRUIT Loops, Sugar Pops, and apple sauce to eat in the tent. Also granola bars, honeybuns, chips, cookies, and cupcakes.

I'm filling a Styrofoam cup with coffee, when a man announces that thirty minutes from now we heading to the airport. He say the airport has another slot open. With me never bein' in an airport, I didn't know what he mean.

But just like he say, a half hour later, they put us back in helicopters and flew us to Louis Armstrong New Orleans International Airport.

They landed us down at a side building where we entered the airport. Inside, it look like a zoo. To me it had more animals than people: iguana, big dogs, snakes. All kind of animals, except giraffes and hippopotamuses, they didn't have all that.

It was like folks was comin' to town for Big Fat Tuesday, which means Mardi Gras.

I be in the waiting area and the airport people come by and say, "Go to the desk and they tell you where you goin."

At the desk, they told me, "You going to Utah." And I say, "Why we can't go to Texas?"

You look up on the chart and they show how all the states is fill up—the hotels and all. I say, "Who I know in Utah? My family in Texas."

Then the lady say, "Oh, they have space to Washington, D.C. If y'all willing to take that plane, we'll take y'all there." She say it's Delta. I say, "Ma'am I never been on a delta in my life." My homeboy Charles—he know "Delta" means it be a plane.

I say, "Where we gonna go in D.C.?"

Charles say, "Ain't nothing but a hip and a hop from Washington, D.C. to Maryland. Maybe we go there."

The airport lady say they have snacks on the plane. Also she say they have waitress on the plane.

I say, "Nice-lookin' waitress?" I just try to say something to make myself cheered up.

My homegirl Cheryl, she with me too. A lot of us from my area where I come up are gonna be on my plane.

When I get on that plane and walk all the way to the back, I say, "Damn, when the end of this plane gonna come?"

Cheryl, say, "Why you goin' to the back?"

I tell her, "The back more cooler than the front. The front you see everything. I don't want to see that."

The waitress say Cheryl can't sit on my lap. She say you gotta sit in your own seat with a seatbelt.

The plane took off and headed into the clouds; it be dark and remind me of what we just been through all over again. And now it went back to my mind about that plane that crashed in the '80s.

But there was no turning backwards now. I was on my way, leaving my hometown for another state. I wonder how it gonna feel bein' in another state where I don't know anyone. Good part is I'll be with a better roof over my head, not eatin' cold sandwiches, no more water in the streets, no more nightmares. I'm dreamin' of hot food and a dry place to live.

Well, that's not how it turned out.

28

SOME PEOPLE HAD LITTLE BITTY DOGS ON THE plane. Blind people had they big dogs. It bein' like Noah's Arc with all the hamsters, parrots, iguanas, and snakes.

Once we got relaxed, the Delta waitress come around and offer you water, soda, peanuts, sandwiches. They told us to let one of them know if we want to use the bathroom, otherwise stay seated when the plane bein' moved. No electronics, which we didn't have anyway. A lot of us had a suitcase, though, and pictures of family.

The waitress showed me how to push a button to make the back of my seat move. I closed my eyes and all them dogs on the plane got me thinkin' 'bout Bundy.

Bundy—one of my friends' dogs—was the baddest dog around. He don't lose. Last dog I seen him fight, he killed that dog; it was really no fight. Bundy's owner feed him raw steak and raw chicken. He take all the bones out because bones choke in the throat.

Bundy look like a body-building dog. He stay chained up underneath the projects with a mask on his mouth. During the past weeks, he and his owner ain't nowhere to be found. I can tell you one thing, though. Wherever Bundy go, he win the show. You can put your house up on Bundy and you ain't gonna lose it.

The police couldn't even touch the master without Bundy goin' off.

Bundy was a dog that seek and destroy. When I see Bundy lock up on another dog, I say Oh my God, you dead. *Sometimes Bundy had a lock on them but they didn't die.*

They fight under the table, because it against the law to do the dogfight. But you know people do what they do. Some young kids come along thinking they got a bad dog.

Bundy's owner don't go lookin' for fight. Bundy even have a sweet nature. He'll let a kid wrassle with him, pull his collar, ride on his back. Bundy never snap at a kid.

If someone come with their dog to fight, Bundy's master say, "You sure you want your dog to fight my dog? Bundy might put a damage on him." Whatever Bundy owner say, Bundy listen.

I had some boys in my neighborhood, who could steal dogs, even Bundy. They come and say you think your dog can't get taken? And you say, no, you can't take him.

Bundy's owner Kevin—we called him Kid—had to pay those boys to get Bundy back.

When I see Bundy fight, I just say to myself, That other dog about to die today. I don't know why the others come around. *I think,* Please get this dog away. *But I admit I be cheerin' for Bundy 'cause he gonna put in work.*

Of course, it put chills in me that the dogs shouldn't fight. I don't like to see no animal get bruised. But I'm only a guest watching a dog fight; there's so many going on. It's just part of life in the projects.

The plane makes a jolt and bounces me back to knowin' I'm way up in the sky.

29

ON THE PLANE, YOU GOT SANDWICH SMELL, DRUNK people smell, cat smell, dog smell. It smell like between McDonald's and a pet store. You got some little birds, makin' little bird noises up with the luggage. One dude got a iguana on each shoulder. You could hear dogs growling, little bitty Chihuahuas squeakin'. One lady had a big ol' zipper bag with a turtle in it.

A man say we on a 747, and I thought, *Wow, we goin' in style, like the President fly.*

I look around and people starin' at they family pictures, and not too much talkin'. Not that we couldn't talk or nothin', but people praying, lookin' out the window, mumblin' to theyself. One guy singin' gospel. The more the plane goin' into the clouds, the more worried I be gettin'.

Bein' next to the window, I open the little shade and watch the sky gettin' real dark. I couldn't sleep, because with me never bein' that high before, I worry what gonna happen.

The waitress comin' around askin' if we need anything. I put in my mind why should I be scared when this female waitress askin' these questions? I told my homegirl, "It like the old song lyric, 'Fly like the eagle into the sea.'" It built my courage up to think about flyin' like a eagle.

I started to talk, tried to motivate everybody around me, tellin' them, "We come this far, we gonna make it." Actually, I be tryin' to convince myself.

Then a man's voice say, "Attention everyone." I look around for him. I thought he be right there. But I couldn't see him. He on a loudspeaker. He say, "It's not too long until we reach our destination and the plane be landing."

I said to myself, *How they gonna land this big ol' plane?* The waitress was telling me we gonna drop—it may hit your stomach a little bit.

I say, "Why it gonna do something to my stomach?" And I think, *Oh Lord.*

I fake sleep so I don't feel it. I put the blanket over my head and worry how it gonna hit my body like *boom* when we land. When I hear the waitress passing by, I stick my head out and ask her, "How this go?"

Talking to the lady made me feel better. I asked her, "How long you been workin' on this plane?" All kind of question to take my mind off thoughts of this plane crashing.

Now that we about to land, all I feel is sudden jerking. Cheryl sitting next to me. I got my head on her shoulder, and she got her head against mine.

I see the plane coming down and then come the *BOOM*. We bounce and we be landed. It hit my stomach in a way I never felt before.

I say, "I hope the brakes on this plane good, 'cause we still like we flyin', but on the ground."

I'm thinking, *What's gonna happen now?*

30

NOW THAT I'M IN WASHINGTON, D.C., I LOOK OUT the window and everything startin' to be new, even before I unbuckle my seat belt.

I feel excited and I feel afraid. I'm curious to get off the plane and out to the airport. What this new life gonna be like?

I hope D.C. at least remind me something of my hometown. I hope the food gonna be like in New Orleans, especially the chicken.

I hope they find us a good place to sleep.

I hope they let us see doctors to check on our health.

I hope I meet up with some of my family, that maybe didn't go to Texas.

I hope they give us some clothes.

I wonder how the time run. Do it be daylight here? I thought it might be dark most of the day here, because

I never been to another state before.

As soon as we got into the airport from the Delta plane, we heard shouts of "Congratulations," shouts of "Praise God." It was a crowd of people, cheering like we was celebrities.

The way they was greetin' us, it seemed they had good folks here, some with volunteer badges, some Red Cross, some military in uniform.

We walked out of the airport to what looked like hundreds of busses, and I caught a flashback to all them National Guard trucks lined up at the projects to help folks get out of New Orleans.

I asked, "What are all them busses out there. Is this a bus station too?"

They tell me the busses was waiting for Katrina victims. We loadin' you up, they say. Those busses gonna take you to the Armory.

"What?" I asked. "We stayin' at a army base?"

A Metro police say to me, "You gonna be all right." He told me they got food and beds and there's health care in a trailer."

They makin' sure nobody in serious pain. That right there put a smile on my face. But I still be wonderin', *Who I gonna run into that I know? I really want to run into Calio and KK.*

They squashed us into them busses, and then drive a whole parade of busses across a bridge. They say that at the Armory there'll be a big gate that will open for us. It make me think of prison.

From me bein' in prison, I was thinking, *Now's my chance to get a new life, if they don't hold my past in New Orleans against me.*

31

THERE WAS MORE BUSSES TAKING US TO THE Armory than there are people at the Mardi Gras Zulu parade in New Orleans. That gotta be a lotta people.

Ah we had fun at Mardi Gras! I can't leave my hometown story without sayin' what that like.

Fat Tuesday is the main day of Mardi Gras. There are a lot of parades. At the Zulu parade, my favorite, you get coconuts. Most people that tour come to get the coconuts and take them home to put on they mantle for souvenir.

Mardi Gras was my best part of the year. You could see everybody you wanna see. Old school friends, old teachers, kids. Everybody come out.

Me bein' the type of guy I was in the street, if I don't see my buddies for Mardi Gras, I know they either locked up or dead. They would say the same about me.

People in the hospital would sneak out, at least I would, to go to Mardi Gras. That's how much I love it.

You see people getting drunk, sleepin' on the curb, sleepin' in they car, and *on* they car. You try different liquor. Too much excitement.

When I was around ten, I was curious about the bar where strippers be at. During the day, we would get away with drinking there—T.J. Swann, our favorite cheap wine with flavors like "Stepping Out" and "Magic Moments." But there be no strippers at the bar during the day. At night we weren't allowed in, but we could peep through a crack in the door if the bouncer step away.

You can find all kind of different drugs at Mardi Gras. You meet all kind of people. You get undercover police acting like they drunk. One year at Mardi Gras, me and my friends need money for drugs so bad we not thinkin' straight.

We meet this guy on the street. He say he from out of town, and he trying to cop some weed. I say, "You got the weed right here. How much you want?'

He say "I want a ounce bag but I'll spend more than that if it's good."

With me bein' a city slicker, and with me and my friend bein' so high, we just thinkin' about the money, we didn't think he be a cop. So I went around the corner and pick up a leaf off the ground and tear it up like weed and put it in a bag.

I go back and tell him, "I been in prison. I know if I hand it to you, it be distribution. It be better if I put it on the ground here, then it's only possession."

He say, "Aw man I'm not no cop, I'm just trying to get high." He wearing Mardi Gras beads, in all different colors. He really had me fooled. He look like a Hawaiian guy or Spanish or Creole. Also, he had a accent which throw me off.

So when he takes out his wallet, and starts pullin' out bills, I see nothin' but money—twenties, fifties, hundreds. My eyes went back in my head when I saw all that cash.

I say to myself *I'm about to get so high now. I got me one.* It's like I got a duck. So I tell him, "You can't pull the money out here man, the cops will see us."

"So," he say, "let's step in the thrift shop." So we standin' inside this shop surrounded by silverware, costumes, beads, all kind of stuff.

While we in there, I notice a lady outside the door shakin' her head at the guy. I say to my buddy, "This guy about to be a police. We goin' to jail."

I set the fake weed on a shelf. When I reach for the money, he show me his badge. At the same time he talkin' into his shirt. It gotta be a microphone in there.

When my buddy and I tried to go out the door, the lady from across the street and other police box us in. They walk us around to the police station near Bourbon Street.

I told my buddy I had an instinct the guy be a cop, but then I seen all that money—and I thought we hit the goldpot.

They handcuff us to a chair and escort us to jail in a transport truck. After that we got booked for possession of marijuana. They arrest a lot of people at Mardi Gras, so the cell was full. There ain't really no room for us, but they squeeze us in.

We spent four days there, until they come in the cell and tell us the DA did not accept the charge. He tell us they sent the "weed" to the lab and it wasn't nothin' but leaves.

So I and my buddy roll out the next day.

With me bein' a hustler, Bourbon Street is where I would go every day, because you always have people slippin'. They drunk and you can talk them out of somethin'. Scam artists from everywhere know about Bourbon Street.

You got hustlers from up North go to Mardi Gras and Bourbon Street to hustle. You even got advertising by fake lawyers. They'll give you a card with they phone number but they ain't gonna be there. They tell you they get you out in thirty minutes. They hustle the hustlers.

I used to like jumpin' up on a float to snatch beads or other things. We give the beads to girls and tell them, "Pretty pearls for pretty girls."

Now that I'm older and more focus, I see things different. I wish I could turn back the hands of time, but it's a done deal. I have no problem today sharing with anyone or helping anyone or mentor with anyone, because I like to give back. I wouldn't want to get paid for it. I just like leading others to a better life.

Epilogue

*F*OR NINE YEARS AFTER *HURRICANE* *KATRINA* AND *bein' evacuated to D.C., things was kinda rough. It was a lot of faults I was makin'. But then things really turn around for me.*

May 7, 2014. You can't forget the date when you do something bad. I was subpoena to go in front of the judge for missing two urine tests.

I was really nervous about going to court. All kind of negative thoughts came to mind, like maybe I be sent back to prison, 'cause I knew my urine be dirty.

My friend Miss Edrie Irvine and my editor, Susan Orlins, came to court that morning. My eyes tear up, because I didn't want these people, who mean a lot to me, to hear I done bad things, like taking drugs. But now I know they my true friends—they still stay with me.

I was especially mad that day when the judge told me I had to go to a drug treatment program.

The parole officer said I should be in jail till the program get a bed space. But after my lawyer hand the judge twenty-two pages—all the recommends from my customers and a picture of me and my editor getting interviewed on TV—the judge took a fifteen-minute break.

She come back and stated she read over the recommends. I think the judge felt I do something for society and that we all deserve a second chance. She give a ruling for me to stay in society until they got a bed space at the program.

I clapped my hands under the table, because I wanted to be free. I didn't want to see jail at all.

After court that morning, me and my lawyer talk. I told him I appreciate him for helping me stay out in society until I go in the program. He asked me do I think I could make it through the program without getting in trouble.

I told him, "I ain't got no other choice because I don't want to go back to jail." And he said, "I hope you do right man, because you got a lotta people pulling for you."

More than anything, I didn't want to let the people down who supported me. I never had this many people

I can open up with. That's what I believed would keep me focus. They are people who accept me for who I be.

That day in court it give me the strength that I have friends to sit in with me. When I used to go to court I didn't really have no support. That also lets the judge know you have folks that care for you.

Eleven months later . . . April 13, 2015. This morning I got in the courtroom for a status hearing on my last urinalysis.

Nearly a year ago I entered Phoenix House for a residential drug treatment program. I didn't wanna be there. But I didn't wanna go back to jail neither.

In the program, I went to group meetings eight hours a day. You speak out about your problems, you write about your triggers. Some guys who spoke out, their stories was like mine. The counselors tell you to build your network with positive people and open up if something bothers you.

It was all nerve-wracking to me. I wanted to run away, but if I run, I be sent back to prison. It was like Monopoly: if I leave the place, I pass go and get sent directly to jail. I would not collect two hundred dollars; instead, I would collect sixty months.

Only some meetings inspired me. But one morning, after saying my prayer, full reality set in. I say to myself, I risked so many years with chemicals in my body and now all these people want to help. I decided to stay focus, to pull myself together.

I began talking out at meeting. And I reached out to help others. I could feel things was changing for me. I thought about all I had going on before the program and how I could be more focus now, like with my writing, and I felt like if I use the tools I learned in the drug program, I should not fall.

Because of my progress, I was permitted to move ahead of schedule to a recovery house, where I live with nine other men, all who had problems like I had. Knowing I had a rent to pay, that make me manage the money I earn from selling my papers. As required for staying in the recovery house, I went to NA meetings every day for thirty days. I continue to go to meetings.

So here I was, back in court on April 13, 2015. I faced the same judge I went in front of the year before—the one who sentenced me to the drug program.

The judge called on the parole officer and asked what the report was since the last time I been in, and the PO say everything good and my urine clean.

The judge feel so good about it, she smiled. I smiled. And then she ask the lawyer do he have anything to say.

He say, "No your honor, I'm proud of Mr. Anderson."

And then the judge ask me do I have anything to say, and I say, "Yes ma'am, your honor.

She say go on and say what you've got to say.

And I say, "Thank you, Judge, for giving me a second chance," and she say you're welcome. She also say let me know when your book come out.

Hearing the judge say that make me smile. She say every *Street Sense* paper that come out she buys it. She want to buy my book! And she proud of me. She say she showed my stories from *Street Sense* to her family.

I had to put my head down and smile. It make me feel proud compared to what judges used to say to me.

Also everything got dismissed on me, meaning I don't have to go in front of the court no more, except for one final time, lessen I get in trouble. I felt so good. I know that six months from now, when I go back in front of the judge with the same good behavior, I really feel to believe she'll take me off supervision entirely.

ACKNOWLEDGMENTS

FIRST OF ALL, I LIKE TO THANK GOD.

I thank Miss Edrie Irvine for her support through good times and bad times and for keeping me strong and focus, which I still am today.

I thank all my *Street Sense* customers for their support and help and for being like family to me.

I thank *Street Sense* for allowing me to be a vendor and share my story: Willie Schatz, Kate Sheppard, Bryan Bello, Sue Dorfman, Brandon Caudill, Jeff Gray, Brian Carome, Eric Falquero, and all the Media Lab, staff, and volunteers

I thank Phoenix House—the staff, the medical, and everyone in the NA meetings—for working with me and giving me advice to help me stay focus. I thank the sponsors, who inspired me with their stories of recovery.

I thank Lily Thneah for taking the time out to shoot such good pictures for my book. Her being so generous means a lot to me.

I thank Bonnie Rich for all the time and trouble it took to make a great video. I really had fun working with Bonnie down by the courts and also where I sell my papers and talk to customers.

I thank Bryan Bello and the Street Sense Media Lab filmmakers for working with me and making a great video and bringing back my memories of New Orleans.

I thank Linda Gerson, who didn't even know me, for helping make my website.

I thank Willie Schatz, Elissa Parker, Kawin Wilairat, Anita Bernstein, Sam Stern, and Eliza Orlins for reading my book and liking it and making suggestions.

I thank Kate Sheppard, Sue Dorfman, Jill Dykes, Mark Matthews, Alexander Jacobs, Sue Katz Miller, Gail Leondar-Wright, and Kathy Slobogin for their advice about promoting the book.

I thank my roommate, Chuck Clemens, for all his help and friendship.

I thank Carolyn Sheltraw for making the book look so good.

I thank Miriam's Kitchen, DCJCC's Theatre J, and also Bill Greene for reading and acting out my story so good, and I thank everyone who came out to see "Homeless Lives: Unforgettable Personal Stories."

I thank the producers of "Let's Talk Live" and especially Kellye Lynn for interviewing me on television.

I thank Charles Carson for how good he explained my way of talking.

I thank Steve Sawyer for his kindness.

I thank Susan Orlins for being my friend, my editor, and someone I can talk to about anything.

This book wouldn't be possible without many of those I thanked above and the decision by Judge Deborah Robinson, who leave it open for me to go to a program instead of prison. I can't wait to sign my book for her and everyone else.